UNDERSTANDING ~ *the* ~ HEAVENS

A Balanced and Biblical Guide to Spiritual Warfare

CURTIS WILSON

ISBN 978-1-68517-875-8 (paperback)
ISBN 978-1-68517-876-5 (digital)

Copyright © 2022 by Curtis Wilson

All rights reserved. No part of this publication may be reproduced, distributed, or transmitted in any form or by any means, including photocopying, recording, or other electronic or mechanical methods without the prior written permission of the publisher. For permission requests, solicit the publisher via the address below.

Christian Faith Publishing, Inc.
832 Park Avenue
Meadville, PA 16335
www.christianfaithpublishing.com

Printed in the United States of America

INTRODUCTION

*Therefore, I run thus: not with uncertainty. Thus,
I fight not as one who beats the air.*

—1 Cor 9:26

Imagine seeing a boxing match where one of the contestants is swinging wildly into the air, leaving it to chance if he connects with his opponent. We would have to think that perhaps he needs to go back and learn some things. It is in this context that I would like to offer a balanced approach to the fight that is before us. As the church moves into the end of the age, it will be more critical than ever that we understand the realm of the spirit and our part to play as believers. It would stand to reason that if I am aware and have a good understanding of my adversary and the battlefield, the outcome could possibly change in my favor or at least help me mentally prepare for the fight. The goal of this series of teachings is to enlighten you and give you the assurance that Christ is all in all when it comes to spiritual warfare. I believe that Christ has the power and authority to keep you no matter how challenging the conflict gets.

Being God's minister for well over twenty years has allowed me to have observation into several instances that could have had a different outcome or perhaps been avoided all together if the people involved might have applied the information about to be presented. These teachings are birthed from a heart to see the Lord's people stand in the midst of a generational onslaught of evil, wickedness, and perversion. Behind this author's fingertips are the memories of those who became casualties of the spiritual war that will continue until Christ's return. My prayer for you is that these writings will effectively put into your hands the tools that allow you to lead a victorious and overcoming life. Most of all, I pray that your relationship with the Lord gravitates to a deeper place than ever before.

RCW (June 15, 2021)

PREFACE

When it comes to spiritual warfare, there are three predominant entities engaged in the battle against you. These are the flesh, the world, and Satan. Each of these have a distinct part to play, and the Lord will equip us to combat each of these as we follow Him. In this teaching, we will attempt to illustrate the things that make up the threefold cord of warfare coming against us. At first glance, this can appear to be a stacked deck, but no worries, God has the winning hand. Our assignment is to make sure we continue to enjoy the Father access bought and paid for at the cross of Calvary.

As a sidenote of clarification, you must remember that the attack is against the King and His kingdom. Unless this point is established, the lines can be blurred significantly. It is not your personal kingdom that the enemy wants to destroy. As a matter of fact, they would love to help you maintain your personal kingdom. No, the real conflict is designed to keep you from making a connection with God Himself and surrendering to *His* kingdom. This threefold attack has one purpose in mind, to destroy your trust and personal relationship with the Lord. As Job's wife said in the Old Testament, "Curse God and die!" (Jb 2:9).

If the enemy can get you to turn from God rather than to God, then Christ's gift of redemption, that is to give you access to God Himself, would be of no effect. Sometimes, it is easy to forget the importance of the entry we have to this throne of grace as born-again believers. It is this access that allows God's power and peace to flow into our lives. Hopefully, we can keep that in our minds as we continue to engage the enemy of our soul. It is only by going into God that you and I have the ability to endure circumstances and enjoy this journey of life.

One other thought as we venture into the realm of spiritual warfare: you are only a piece of the puzzle. You are like a tile in the great mosaic story that God has been writing for generations. This certainly does not diminish your importance in that story. After all, God sent His only son to die in our place. But it does help us to remember that we are always entering into other's work as well as paving the way for future generations. It is with this eternal view in our hearts that this book is written. Our desire is that future generations of Christ-like followers would develop a sense of belonging to something greater than themselves. It is this purpose and calling of kingdom that we speak of. It is this greater good and kingdom-mindedness that will allow our lives to speak into the darkness of the human heart.

Although I walk through the valley of the shadow of death, I will fear no evil; For you are with me.

—Psalm 23:4

CHAPTER 1

A THREEFOLD CORD

Ecclesiastes 4:12 says, "A threefold cord is not easily broken." In this chapter, we will give an overview of this threefold cord against us and break down some particular aspects of each. In later chapters, we will build upon this platform and attempt to illustrate some of the ways we become intertwined in the war. This overview is important to establish your understanding of the heavenlies. Each of us tend to approach this subject with a premeditated view. A lot of information has been cast on us in the last century about the battlefronts, battlegrounds, and opponents. By concreting this overview in your heart, at this juncture, we hope to make this subject of spiritual warfare fresh and personal.

The first foe we must be aware of when engaging in the battle is our flesh. It is what I sometimes label as "friendly fire." That is because each of us have grown accustomed to it, nursed it, and have helped it along the way. The flesh is simply our carnal man or what is referred to in Scripture as the natural man (1 Cor 2:14). The origin of our flesh nature comes from the third chapter of Genesis when man and woman decided to disobey God's command to not eat the fruit of the Tree of the Knowledge of Good and Evil. From this experience came a windfall of challenges and engaged all of us in the battle. The one thing you must comprehend in order to combat the flesh is that anything it has to offer is worthless. It is completely useless to fight this war because it is constantly trying to take what only belongs to God. This point is illustrated in the fourth chapter of Genesis when Cain and Abel brought offerings to the Lord. At some point, you must quit trying to dress up the dog and come to terms with the fact that Jesus wants self to be terminated! This isn't always a clean process, but here are some things to check when making decisions each day whether to fulfill the lusts of the flesh or walk in the Spirit (Gal 5:16).

Motivation. Why am I making this decision? Is it something God has inspired, or does it feed my natural man by giving it security or significance? The statement Jesus made in Luke 16:13 that we can have only one Master applies to this area of our lives. *Mammon* is not just a term for money but the constant pull of self-life that competes with the will of God for my time.

Energy. By what means is this idea being fueled? I have personally seen many believers, through the years, that were burned out in their efforts to get the "work of the Kingdom" accomplished. Truth is that when the Holy Spirit gives you the energy/grace to fulfill what He is directing, you are a much more restful person. Work in the Kingdom comes from a place of rest (Heb 4).

When Jesus said to pick up our cross and follow, He knew that dying to self was the remedy for our flesh nature. As believers, we have been given the Holy Spirit as a guide to walk us through the process and navigate our daily experiences. Sometimes it is hard to distinguish between what is of God and what is not. Which helps us to transition to the next opponent in this spiritual war between light and dark…the world.

When New Testament writers speak of the world through the biblical lens, it is not necessarily this sphere of dirt they have in mind but rather a set of systems that can potentially rule over our lives.

The world's system is designed to deceive its inhabitants into a thought process that is in contradiction to God's word in part or whole. Where the church runs into problems is when we begin to take on worldly principles and adopt them as part of our culture. I would think that if the world outside of the church is no longer offended by the church, we may have adopted some worldly principles.

UNDERSTANDING THE HEAVENS

Scripture teaches that God's ways are higher and completely different from the of man. He can sometimes direct us in a way that might seem contradictory to my human reasoning. Even the Lord's method for salvation is completely foolish in human terms (1 Cor 1:18). This confounding of the carnal mind is perhaps just another reason for us to come to Him constantly for counseling and guidance.

The world's system is a very deceptive tool that can be used to destroy our relationship with God; therefore, the Lord has given us His Holy Scriptures to act not as a legalistic rulebook but a set of precepts to base our beliefs on. Second Timothy 2:15 tells us to rightly divide the word of truth.

Scripture is designed to weave itself into our minds for right thoughts and eventually into our hearts to produce correct character. It is this four-part process found in 2 Timothy 3:16 that produces Christ's character in us. The Bible gives us the knowledge of these "higher" or different ways of God. As we study God's word, we study God Himself. This understanding of the character of God helps when dealing with this next enemy we will consider.

The origin of an age-old spiritual battle that precedes you and me is the discussion for our last topic, and that is Satan. The term *Satan* in Scripture means simply "adversary." Jesus said he was a murderer from the beginning and the father of lies (John 8:44). It stands to reason that deception is his most predominant weapon against us.

Satan is in direct rebellion against God and appears from Scripture to direct an army of demonic spirits. For the sake of time, we will keep this on the surface and perhaps dig into the subject in other teachings.

Satan has one goal in mind, and that is to take the place of the one true God (Is 14:12–14).

One thing to remember about our enemy is that he cannot function in the light. He may appear to be light, but he is immobilized by the truth of God's word and the light that comes from Christ. As long as we are transparent before the Lord, Satan has no power or dominion over us. It is in darkness that Satan and every demon spirit resides. Just the knowledge of this information should compel us to have a love for truth and light.

Let's take a second to review this threefold cord coming against us and be sure you understand that we have the antidote for each one.

1. *The Flesh.* Our path to freedom is found in the cross and allowing our self to be removed so the new nature can thrive.
2. *The World.* As we seek to know God through His word, we will develop a discernment for the information that comes to our minds each day.
3. *Satan.* We should develop an affinity towards exposure. Bringing everything to the light gives Christ the ability to advocate for us.

We will expound the subject of understanding the heavens over the next several teachings, but this will give us some directive and clarity to the battle we are all facing.

Father, I pray for the reader to be enlightened but not overwhelmed by the subject matter of Spiritual Warfare. It is not the enemy that we as believers are focusing on but the One True King of Glory, Your Son, Jesus Christ. May His name be forever on our minds, in our hearts, and on our lips. To this end, we give Him praise in the Highest. Hosanna! Amen.

CHAPTER 2

WALLS AND BRIDGES

But now in Christ Jesus you who once were far off have been brought near by the blood of Christ. For he himself is our peace, who has made us both one and has broken down in his flesh the dividing wall of hostility by abolishing the law of commandments expressed in ordinances, that he might create in himself one new man in place of the two, so making peace, and might reconcile us both to God in one body through the cross, thereby killing the hostility. And he came and preached peace to you who were far off and peace to those who were near. For through him we both have access in one Spirit to the Father.

—Ephesians 2:13–18

As we see from this passage, Christ has done all He can to reconcile us to the Father. Access to the throne of grace has been provided through the cross. This point will be reiterated throughout our teachings because I believe it to be the single most important tool you have for understanding the Heavens. It is also the one thing that cannot be taken from you (Lk 10:42).

If God has provided you with the ability to communicate one on one with His Spirit, why is it that so few believers seem to utilize this crucial aspect of our redemption?

This next segment of our teaching will shed light on what the Scripture term *enmity* or *wall of hostility* is all about. We will begin with a look at barriers and what the demolition of these can look like when the cross is applied to our lives.

The first of these walls we will tear into is the separation of humanity and God due to the law.

Before we go any further it is helpful to keep in mind that the law itself is holy and good. The problem comes in because man cannot keep the law, and this creates a wall of separation called sin. The penalty of sin, which is isolation from God, has been removed in Christ. But the old nature continues to obstruct our view and actually causes us to not do the very thing that our spirit knows to do, and that is to come before God. You see the old nature, which the flesh is accustomed to, gets its roots from the law. Although the law of God has always existed, it was not imputed to man until he consumed of the fruit from the Tree of the Knowledge of Good and Evil. It was at this moment that the ability to comprehend God's law was available to humanity. And this is where the root of our problem as believers in Christ comes in. You see we cannot mix the keeping of the law and the grace given by the finished work of Calvary. As a matter of fact, these two are in direct opposition to one another. The law and grace is a volatile combination when housed in the same vessel. Because these are so toxic to each other, one of them must exit. I thought we could take the time to compare these two and gain understanding of what each provide.

1. The law brings death, but the Spirit brings life abundantly (2 Cor 3:6). When we depart from the spirit walk, the journey begins to feel isolated and confusing. When we walk in the spirit, the Lord gives vitality to every situation. It is the presence of God's Spirit that allows us to enjoy a vigorous life.
2. The law breeds condemnation, but grace justifies you before God (Heb 9:14–15). Condemnation, in biblical terms, is the ability to judge a situation and determine the outcome. The nature of our carnal man is to reason everything out, but this oftentimes produces bondage in areas of our lives. We must come to terms with reality. In Christ

you have been set free. When we walk in the Spirit, our lives become marked by freedom.
3. The law works to keep its place, but grace receives an inheritance through adoption (Rom 8:14–15). There is nothing you can do to earn this inheritance. In Christ, we have been grafted into the family. This truth is powerful when it finally takes root in our hearts. Our lives then become more about who we are than what we do.
4. The law promotes unbelief and fear, but grace lifts us to a supernatural experience with God through faith (Rom 4:20). Life in the spirit gives us a trust in God that all things and every situation must pass through Him. It is this trust that enables us to walk through every circumstance with the attitude that it will eventually work out for good (Rom 8:28).
5. The law puts demands on us, but grace supplies all we need by His Spirit (Phil 4:19). God is the ultimate Father. As a father, I would never give my children an assignment that did not come with the proper training or supplies. Trust that the Lord will give you everything needed to fulfill His purposes for you. This is the lesson that Israel learned over a forty-year stretch in the wilderness. The end of their journey was marked with praise and trust in the God who supplies (Nm 21:17).

Receiving the revelation that we have become a new creation in Christ and that old things have passed away, let us move on to building bridges into God's presence (2 Cor 5:16–21). After all, this is the greatest asset we have and the one thing that is continually fought against.

On my dad's side of my family, we go back three generations of men that worked in the industry of building bridges. I grew up with a pretty good understanding of the construction process of building a bridge no matter the size or expanse that has to be crossed.

The first order of business in building any bridge is the approach. The way we approach God's presence is always the same no matter what emotional state we happen to be in at that moment. You see, once I realized that Christ has done what we could never do by giving us this access, it created a complete change in attitude. Just the knowledge of what God has done on our behalf should give us a posture of gratefulness. Being thankful in a world that is steeped in unthankful can sometimes get us confused but this is why the Lord instituted the Eucharist, or what most evangelicals call Communion. The Communion meal was instituted for us to always remember Christ's sacrifice and the privilege of being born again (2 Cor 11:23–26).

This leads us to another part of the bridge-building process that isn't so obvious. You see when you build a bridge, you never start on one side and go across. You always start from each side and work toward each other. God has made the way but allows us the freedom to access Him at any given time. The best part about coming to God is that He will meet you more than halfway. It is in the nature of our heavenly Father to draw near to us as we draw near to Him. Never think that the Lord isn't as delighted to see you and have a relationship with you as you are to Him. The whole purpose for the cross was to bring us in as part of the family.

The Holy Spirit shared this principle with me when our oldest daughter was a toddler. We had several people, all for different reasons, living with us during this time. As a retreat, my wife and I would often go into the master suite and read, watch TV, or visit with each other. When someone would need us, they would usually come to the door and knock. Everyone but our daughter, Racheal. She would, without hesitation, come flying into the room with whatever joy, problem, or new story she had on her mind. It was at one of these moments that the Lord gave me the revelation of how we should be with Him. You see there is no need to be timid when we approach the throne of grace. This is what the author of the book of Hebrews considers as boldness to approach (Heb 4:16). God is a loving Father that desires the relational aspect of your redemption as much as we do.

We will look at some of the tools designed to help you in our next lesson, but I want to conclude by saying, "Enter into an intimate relationship with God." It is the single most important thing you can do as a believer in Jesus Christ and the greatest benefit we have in understanding the heavens. Our personal relationship with God is the thing that separates Christianity from all other religions. It is where you will find personal fulfillment and a joy that surpasses anything this world can offer.

Father, we ask that you give us a supernatural understanding of our inheritance in Christ. That the old letter of the law may be eradicated, and the new creation emerge. As we come before you with joy, confidence, and praise let us be reminded of the overwhelming sacrifice you made to get us to this place. May each of us draw near to where you are and look for the day when we can see you face to face. But until that day, let each of us enjoy living this day in your presence, AMEN.

CHAPTER 3

STRONGHOLDS

Now I, Paul, myself am pleading with you by the meekness and gentleness of Christ—who in presence am lowly among you, but being absent am bold toward you. But I beg you that when I am present I may not be bold with that confidence by which I intend to be bold against some, who think of us as if we walked according to the flesh. For though we walk in the flesh, we do not war according to the flesh. For the weapons of our warfare are not carnal but mighty in God for pulling down strongholds, casting down arguments and every high thing that exalts itself against the knowledge of God, bringing every thought into captivity to the obedience of Christ, and being ready to punish all disobedience when your obedience is fulfilled.

—2 Corinthians 10:1–6

stronghold
- A fortified place;
- A place of security or survival;
- A place dominated by a particular group or marked by a particular characteristic.

The combination of Scripture and this *Webster's* definition leads us to a conclusion that for our study today, strongholds are simply a dwelling place of darkness within our souls where God has not been enthroned. It is possibly a fortified retreat for our carnal man to stay in charge of certain decisions, actions, and areas of our lives. If left unchecked, these areas can become a major stumbling block on our way to living a life of newness and freedom in Christ.

The good news is, the Lord wants you to be free from strongholds. The bad news is, self will have to let go of some territory.

Some Examples of Strongholds from Scripture

Traditions/Beliefs (John 3). Nicodemus had a stronghold that affected his ability to fully comprehend who Jesus was and the kingdom principles being taught. Time and time again, we see that our belief system dictates the choices we make. It is a spiritual truth that you will never act consistently against your belief system. This is what the Scriptures refer to as the heart of a person. It is out of the heart that not only our mouth speaks, but our actions are defined by the issues of the heart. It is the part of the redemptive plan for you and me to be changed. As we grow in our knowledge and experience with the Lord, our heart is transformed to reflect the image of Christ.

Wealth (Luke 18). The rich, young ruler had his security in the things of this world. Remember that wealth can be defined as the abundance of earthly goods. These are the resources we put assurance in, such as finance, education, credentials, etc. Each of these have a place in our life but can never hold the title of the assurance. That position is reserved for God alone. One of my commentators stated that wealth is desired so that we can control the circumstances and establish dominance over those we believe to be subordinate. Abundance can be used to further God's purposes but must not become a barrier to circumvent true repentance or humility. God understands the trappings of wealth and our humanity therefore He needs to remain in authority of our lives.

Part of the reason God refers to Himself as "I Am" several times is to allow for the hearer to put his/her assurance in the one sure thing, "Jesus Christ is the same yesterday, today, and forever" (Heb 13:8).

Relationships (Luke 9:60). Jesus tells a man to "let the dead bury the dead." I believe Jesus is referring to those relationships that take a space that is designed for God alone. He paid the ultimate price for you to have access to the Father. Our desire for spiritual community (which is God-given) can take over a healthy balance to our heavenly relationship. It is possible for these types of relationships to become toxic when they obstruct God's place in your life. Examples could be friends, family, or church leaders. The test for this is, Am I seeking the Lord first? There is nothing wrong with asking advice or counsel from friends, but if it is replacing my relationship with the Lord, I may have a problem.

It is possible to have community without having these relational strongholds that keep you from have the proper relationship with the Lord. True spiritual community, it can be said, is when each of us ascends the mountain of God and provokes others to do the same.

Luke 14:15–24. The parable of the great supper can be understood in a way that clearly defines the obstructive nature of these strongholds. In this parable, Jesus points out that excuses, no matter how viable, are not a pass from doing what He is calling us to. This can become a thin line to walk given that those around us are not malicious in their thoughts or intents most of the time. I have found that it is usually our lack of diligence or desire to relate to God that allows us to be entangled in these strongholds. But be of good cheer because God has a remedy found in the last few verses of Luke 14. This path is and always will be the most direct way to deal with strongholds. It is the path that leads to self being dethroned and God being enthroned.

How God Deals with these Strongholds

He exposes. Light does not have its full effect until it meets darkness. In Him was life, and that life was the light of men (Jn 1:4). The apostle John uses the symbol of light numerous times in his writings. It was John that pointed out how Jesus met with Nicodemus to explain the spiritual change that must take place for the human soul to be transformed. There is a good reason the Bible tells us that Nicodemus came to Jesus at night (Jn 3:2).

Most of us cringe at the thought of God exposing anything in our lives, but it is the start of this process. Exposure comes from three predominate methods the Bible, by the Spirit intuitively, or by His creation. Each of these have a way of exposing the strongholds in our lives or the lives of others. As we read the Scripture, it has a way of illuminating things that we could never see on our own. This could be one of the most powerful weapons we have against darkness. As the Psalmist said, "In your light, we see light" (Ps 36:9). When I was a new believer, this principle was life-changing for me. Understanding that God has my best interest in mind when He exposes helped me to not feel as though I had to grab a fig leaf to cover my sin. Exposure is not God's way of rejecting us but His way of healing what is broken. Until we can comprehend how painful and powerful exposure can be, it is impossible to grow into a person that is free from strongholds.

He assaults. Good thing about walking with the Lord is that He won't just leave you in your vulnerable condition after this exposure. God is faithful to carry you through the process for us to become whole again. His goal is to have you free from strongholds, not to push you away. Because most of us are uncomfortable with conflict, this part of breaking free can become unnerving and just downright uncomfortable. After all, who wants the Lord to assault their stronghold? We either want to avoid having to keep journeying, or we are scared of how the healing will manifest. Those that want to avoid the process of healing usually seek out how they can get an instantaneous fix. This is like a person who wants the latest weight loss machine to keep from having to work out daily to stay healthy. From my view of the New Testament, especially the Gospels, Jesus did not deal with each person the same way. He has been called the Great Physician for this reason. He knows what it will take to free each of us from these strongholds.

The Holy Spirit's power comes in what I see scripturally as two different forms. The first is a life-changing moment that allows us to connect with the eternal power of the Creator. An encounter with God's dynamic power can change our lives forever. Whether physical, mental, or spiritual healing, this form of God's power is something that cannot be mistaken for anything else. We see those times in Scripture that an individual needed to have the Lord intervene in such a way that they could not mistake Him for anything but the Messiah. It is true that He wants to disrupt your situation for His good and for His glory. But this is not always the method He uses to free us from strongholds. The kingdom of God is governed by a set of principles and these principles are also what the Lord uses to establish his dominion in your life. Sometimes it is not a "Power" encounter that we need to set us free. It is that we need to put God's principles to work in our lives on a continual basis. I admit this can be frustrating if we are expecting God to change us instantaneously. You see, as followers of Christ, we must commit to walking out the necessary procedure for our hearts to remain in liberated. Both of these methods have the ability to produce a turning point in our lives and have the power to set you free from strongholds. These are a prerequisite for spiritual growth because believe it or not God's desire is that you become complete. This transitions us into the next point of our teaching.

He sets up dominion. At this point of kingdom dominion, there is an exchange that takes place between your sinful nature and the new nature of Christ. The exchange of dark for light, deception for truth, and bondage for freedom. In that exchange, true freedom and the ability serve others in love comes to the forefront of our lives. Jesus was continually referring to this exchange in dialogue with His disciples. In John 13, there is a recollection by John of their final Passover meal together at which the Lord clothes Himself in a towel and begins to wash feet. The freedom that comes from serving others is how we are designed as new creations in Christ.

It is our rightful place as sons/daughters of the kingdom to enjoy our surroundings. Also, freedom from these strongholds will give you the ability to hold to your traditions/beliefs without them paralyzing revelation, the ability to have earthly things that have no hold on us, and the ability to form relationships that propel us to seek the depths of Christ instead of holding us in a shallow form of Christianity.

CHAPTER 4

DEAD TO THE WORLD AND ALIVE TO CHRIST

Adulterers and adulteresses! Do you not know that friendship with the world is enmity with God? Whoever therefore wants to be a friend of the world makes himself an enemy of God. Or do you think that the Scripture says in vain, "The Spirit who dwells in us yearns jealously?"

—James 4:4–5

In this chapter, we look at another wall or what the Bible refers to as an opposition to God. This next subject could not come for most at a more relevant time. This wall of opposition known in Scripture as the world is based solely through how the information you receive is filtered. The world, as referred to in Scripture, is more than just the ground we walk on. It is a system of principles or thoughts that govern the people and spiritual atmosphere of the earth. As the above passage of scripture states, it is in direct opposition to God's principles and the thoughts that He would have to govern our lives. It is adhering to these worldly principles or ideas that can lead us to error in our thoughts and actions. Because the Bible calls Satan the ruler of this world, his main weapon against the body of Christ are these deceptive ideas directed at our thoughts and at our minds. It is the old nature of our carnal mind that wants to adhere to these wrong ideas based on what it feels, sees, and comprehends. More or less, this barrage of thoughts come to us daily from the world around us. This has only increased as the sources for information have become abundant. Unless we form a hedge around our thought life, we are subject to these deceptions and the fruit that comes from worldly thinking. It is this hedge of protection that we will expound on over the next few paragraphs.

First, let's look at how our belief system is formed and consider the thought that a person will never act against his/her beliefs. It is through this belief system that we make choices and create routines that encompass our daily lives. Most people I've met hardly ever have this belief system challenged. We tend to surround ourselves with relationships that shore up our way of thinking and allow us to live according to our viewpoints. Our belief system is usually one of the things we hardly ever focus on, yet as Christians, it is essential if we are to navigate the bombardment of information that comes to us daily. From childhood, we begin this process of forming a belief system, and it continues to solidify as we mature. God's plan is that His word will at some point intercept any errors we have and allow us to walk in freedom and the peace He provides. There are three primary forms that we draw from that help to form our belief system.

One of these is found within us, and it is called human reasoning. The ability to reason out what is good and what is evil comes due to the sin nature we inherited from Adam and is a direct result of humanity's disobedience to God. Because we have the capability to reason every thought that comes to us, it is easy to get trapped in a humanistic belief system. As children, we take what our parents give us and turn that information into a belief system that is either right or wrong. The word of God, accompanied by the Spirit of God, is a powerful combination to us as believers. We will dive deeper into hearing the voice of the Spirit in later chapters, but for now, let us concentrate on the word and its ability to filter the information received.

The second of these primary ways to form our belief system is the church. Because we have what Romans chapter 1 refers to as an internal knowledge of God, it only makes sense that we would look for some way to understand more of the Creator. Most often we turn to the church for this information. It is God's plan that the church be reflective of His heart and His character to those outside the kingdom. This process works very well unless what is being conveyed about God, His kingdom, and character are not completely accurate. Throughout church history, there has existed a tension between what the church is reflecting to be God and what is really God. Anytime there is major error in the church's doctrine, the Lord is faithful to bring things back to center. This is where access to so much information can cripple us unless we have an absolute to filter it through. That absolute is what I sometimes refer to as the tape measure in the construction of our souls. You see trying to build anything without proper tools can be destructive. Therefore, the Lord has given us an answer to the information overload. He has given us a remedy for this onslaught of worldly thoughts and wrong ideas. This is our resolution for the enmity of worldliness.

You see the third method for gathering thoughts and ideas about God comes from the Scripture. God's word has been given to humanity as an antidote for wrong thinking about the King and His kingdom. In this section, we will look at how the Bible should shape our belief system and allow us to be transformed into the image of Christ. Let us remember not to approach the Scripture as a set of rules or dos and don'ts but in a manner that allows the living word to penetrate our hearts. To do this, we will look at a passage of scripture from the Apostle Paul's letter to his spiritual son Timothy. The background for the letter of Second Timothy is that the young evangelist was being challenged by false teachers coming into the church to sway the believers into erroneous thinking. Paul encourages Timothy to preach the word and to allow the Holy Scriptures to speak for themselves. Because God's word is living and powerful, it can change the human heart and does not require assistance except by the Holy Spirit to convey its meaning. The beauty of the word of God is that you do not need a theology degree to interpret it, only a willing heart and humble spirit. God's word is designed to transform your heart and align your character with that of Christ. There is a method that the Scripture has for producing this outcome and it is found in 2 Timothy 3:16.

> All Scripture is given by inspiration of God, and is profitable for Doctrine, for reproof, for correction, for instruction in righteousness.

There are four key things the Scripture accomplishes that we need to take from this verse. To start with, God's word always exposes our incorrect mindsets and brings them to light. You will see this pattern of exposure throughout our teaching because it is always the Lord's beginning to the problem. God is light, and in Him, there is no darkness. All things must be exposed in order for them to be in subjection to the kingdom. The second is that the Scripture will prove your error. This correction is vital to your path to wholeness. As we read the Bible, it shows us that we have been walking in error to the truth of God. Much like our analogy of the tape measure, the Scriptures will simply show you that you have been missing the mark. The third thing we see from this verse is that the Scripture does not just prove you wrong; His word has the intention of setting you on a path to righteousness.

Something about God's word that should be noted at this juncture—it will never leave you *hopeless*. God's character and His goodness always leave you with hope if you adhere to His plan and follow His path. You see, His path will always lead to freedom from self, sin, and death. Even when it doesn't feel good to your flesh, the Lord's chastening should leave you hopeful. If it doesn't, then it may not be the conviction of God you are feeling but condemnation through the law. (Rabbit Trail)

As you follow the Lord's path to freedom, the word then begins to weave itself into your character and produces habits that will keep you liberated. The best part about God's word, and our fourth takeaway from this verse, is that the Scripture's final resting place would be in your heart and will forever transform your character.

Through the years, I have watched as people are converted to Christ through genuine repentance, baptism, and church attendance.

If they do not take personal initiative and absorb God's word on a regular basis, their lives begin to fall apart. This is the essence of true discipleship. "Be not conformed to the world but be transformed by the renewing of your mind" (Rom 12:2).

Now we should be able to see why the removal of the Scripture is crucial if the enemy is to deceive a whole generation. The Bible is clear that in the last days there will be a generation of very deceived and lawless people on the earth. But it is also clear that there will be, in this same generation, a group of firmly planted believers to act as a weapon against the adversary.

As our ability to obtain information grows throughout society, we as believers should find it imperative to mediate and study God's word. It is the cure for worldliness and confusion that comes from living in an immoral society. The Lord has always been faithful to give us teachers and spiritual leaders, but they should never be a replacement for our personal pursuit for truth.

Father, we come before your word with humble hearts and gracious minds. Let us always remember your faithfulness to correct any errors and your steadfast love that gives us a path to freedom. May the reader of this text be encouraged and equipped to pursue your heart throughout each step of their personal journey. In the beginning was the Word, and that Word was God, Amen.

CHAPTER 5

FATHERED BY GOD

> *"Come out from among them and be separate, says the Lord. Do not touch what is unclean, And I will receive you." and "I will be a Father to you, and you shall be My sons and daughters, Says the Lord Almighty."*
>
> —2 Cor 6:17–18

For this present study, we want to continue along the subject of combatting the world, or rather, the system of worldly information that we are bombarded with in our everyday lives. The Scripture itself can be confusing or irrelevant when we are *not* reading it in tandem with the voice of the Spirit. Because we have to cross this barrier in order to live a life that is separate from the world, it is important that we recognize and submit to God's voice on a consistent basis. I originally wanted to write this chapter on how to hear the voice of God, but after some deliberation, I felt that we should go into more detail than that. Because we live in a society that has seen the family unit disintegrate over several decades, most of us are unfamiliar with the idea of being fathered by God. In a world where masculinity is villainized, feminized, or absent, it stands to reason that having any type of father-figure assists us in life would be unfamiliar to most.

UNDERSTANDING THE HEAVENS

So this is not a chapter to just recognize the voice of God but to also understand His purpose behind where, when, and how He leads.

Let me state that this text is written by someone who believes in a Triune God. I believe that although there is only one God, there are three distinct personalities—the Father, Son, and Holy Spirit—that make up this Godhead. Each of these has a role and function when it concerns the redemption of humanity. Holy Spirit's role is to guide us into all truth, and that truth will bring us liberty. That liberty then gives us the motivation to pursue a relationship with Father God that would have been impossible before the cross of Christ. While this is certainly not an exhaustive list on the work of the Godhead, it gives you an understanding of how all three roles work in harmony to bring us a life that is fathered by God. As we allow Scripture to mold and shape us, we also allow the active voice of the Spirit to give us wisdom, direction, and counsel as we walk through the circumstances of this earthly experience called life.

Most of us would agree that adversity is a part of our earthly experience, but to understand the heart of the Father is to understand the why behind each situation we find ourselves being thrust into. For the purpose of our study, let's put each type of adversity into one of three categories. Each of these has an answer to the why, but more importantly, each of these categories has a window into the character and purposes behind our heavenly Father's intent when it comes to our maturing process. I will exposit a passage in Hebrews for our study on these three categories. This passage is Hebrews 12:1–11 and actually continues on through the chapter's end but we will take the first eleven verses for our study. These three groupings are found in systematic order in this passage and will come to you in the same sequence.

1. The first category in dealing with the adversity we face is sin. Because we live in a world that is opposed to God's standards and holiness, we often find that this opposition called sin creates hardship in our lives. The Bible is very clear that the wage of sin is death. The payoff for living in sin is that instead of our lives being filled with peace

and abundance, they become filled with confusion and lack. When processing the information that comes from the world's system, it is important to allow the voice of the Spirit in conjunction with God's word to point out what God's standard of holiness really is and is not. Because we live in a world that would call good evil and evil good, we should allow God to shepherd our hearts in a way that bring us freedom from sin. Because of the pride that comes from the inherent nature of Adam, we must approach the Lord with a humble spirit and submitted mind. True repentance is always the remedy for ongoing sin in our lives.

2. Second of our categories is God's discipline or what the Scripture refers to in Hebrews chapter 12 as the Lord's chastening. Because the Lord is our Father, He will never abandon us or not try to discipline us. To understand this process is to have a glimpse into His purpose for allowing things to come our way that are not created by sin either directly or indirectly. As the perfect Father, the Lord wants us to grow up into spiritual maturity and has a method for doing so. Once sin has been repented of, it is God's way to put us into what I like to call the School of the Cross. This is where we can really understand our relationship as sons and daughters of the King. This is also where the fathering of God can bear the most fruit in our lives. Because the Lord wants us to have every good gift that comes from above, He is faithful to bring us into a place of maturity so we will be able to operate, steward, and enjoy those gifts without them destroying us.

3. This last category is something most believers either have never thought of or simply do not have a doctrine for, and that is adversity that is created by God's righteousness. You see part of being "fathered" by God is that you are now involved in the family business. That business has two main objectives, redeeming mankind and subduing the enemy. These work together to bring evidence of the kingdom of God here on earth through God's chosen method—the

church. Our future studies will address destroying the works of the enemy directly, but for now, let us remember that God's business is our business if we have confessed Jesus Christ as Lord and Savior. As we go through this life here on earth, it is important for us to always keep in mind that because we have the Light of Christ in us therefore, we are the light to the world around us. Just as Christ was crucified because of who He was and not the things He did, you will also face adversity because of who you are.

If we do not have a mindset for the battle around us, then we are prone to make decisions to alleviate the discomfort that this type of adversity creates. When I realize that my hardship is not the result of sin or God's chastening, I have to conclude that there is a kingdom purpose involved. There are always two questions to ask at this point.

First, "Lord, is there someone who is watching my reaction to this adversity, and can there be redemption released because I have experienced this trial?" Second, "Lord, are You perhaps sowing me into a situation so that Your righteousness can be presented to those that are producing unrighteousness?" Both of these questions help to prepare our hearts for battle and allow us to continually approach the throne of grace, knowing that God is not only for us but wants us to work with Him in the business of advancing His kingdom. The world around us, our flesh, and the lie of the enemy is that if we are serving God, our life should be peaceful, but Jesus said, "Peace I leave to you, not as the word gives do I give you." If the light shines through us, then it will always disturb the darkness. Our next chapter will address some of the specific ways that our enemy will try to keep his position, but as sons and daughters of the kingdom, it is our place to rule over the darkness. It is God's place to give us all we need to do so.

Father, I thank you that we can be your children. It is for this purpose that you called us out of the dark and into the light. We know that without you there is nothing we can do to overcome the challenges of this world. But because you have grafted us into this

CURTIS WILSON

family, we will echo a resounding praise for your faithfulness and allow you to father us through any circumstance. May we be a people who will go forth in peace knowing you are the perfect Father. There is truly no one like you, Lord, amen.

CHAPTER 6

PREPARING FOR WAR

In this chapter we will make a shift from focusing on the things that effect our hearts and minds through the world around us and concentrate on direct engagement with the enemy.

Being in covenant with Jesus Christ has consequences, and one of those is that Satan himself is directly opposed to the kingdom we now represent. By walking in a relationship with the Lord, we are making the choice to have His enemies become our enemies. This battle between the kingdoms of this world and the kingdom of our God has been going on for centuries and will continue until Christ comes again at the end of the age. Although Satan is a created being and does not possess the power to defeat the Lord Himself, he is an ancient foe that is relentless in the ruin of whatever bears the name of Christ on this earth. God could have destroyed Satan from the start of his rebellion but has allowed this to become a part of the overall plan of redemption.

Man's fall in the garden of Eden was not simply a mistake to be cleaned up but part of an overarching strategy to bring humanity into the family of God. From the start, God wanted a people that would rule and reign with Him throughout eternity. This life is only a shadow of the good things that are in store for those that believe in Christ. It is in this context of ruling well that I would like to set up our next teaching. Though we are engaged in a battle with beings that have far greater dominance than our natural man can handle, we have been made a new creation that holds all power and authority inherited through Christ Jesus. Along with that authority, you and I have been given certain gifts or weapons, if you will, to fight this battle. These are not always obvious or seen with the natural eye but are nonetheless, always available to the church. Let's take some time to look at what is available to us and how we utilize these resources.

The first of these weapons of our warfare could possibly be the most central to the battle, and that is prayer. Thousands of volumes have been written on prayer throughout the ages, and Scripture is very clear about its importance. As any military knows, communication is key to winning or losing a battle. Therefore, you and I have to commit to learning to be a people of prayer. In recent years, I have personally developed the habit of listening more than talking when it comes to my communication with God. This doesn't mean that I do not request things or ask questions of the Lord, after all, He is my heavenly Father. It simply means that I have developed a particular routine of listening for Him to give me the answers I need to the specifics.

As we continue in this chapter with our study on warfare, it will become apparent how our prayer lives stand central to our engaging the enemy. Sometimes it is helpful when praying to think of your prayers as bullets being fired from a gun. The more accurate we are in prayer, then the higher the chances of us effectively destroying the enemy. We see from the Gospels that Jesus hits the target every time because He was only praying what had been predetermined by the Father. The key to us hitting the mark is that we should only pray in line with what God has predetermined or decreed (Acts 4:28).

This sounds simple but usually isn't. That is why we must cultivate our relationship with the Lord and submit ourselves to His will. This is the next point or weapon in today's teaching we will address, and that is humility. Yes, humility. It is essential if we are to destroy the works of the enemy that we walk in humility toward God and to those around us. There is a form of false humility Colossians 2:23 speaks of that can cripple by steering us into legalism, but that usually occurs when we think incorrectly about our role in the kingdom. You see, there always exists a healthy tension between how high and how low we regard ourselves. If we move too far to one side of the road on these, we will begin to be deceived by the enemy, thus losing our ability to wage proper warfare. First Peter 5:5–10 tells us that when we humble ourselves under the dominion of God, it creates a chain of events that lead ultimately to a victory for the kingdom. Sometimes we get to a place where pride, even in small amounts, begins to distort our view and clog our spiritual ears. When this happens, it is the right time to accompany our prayer with biblical fasting.

This then becomes the third weapon for our arsenal in spiritual warfare. I use the term *biblical fasting* because, in Scripture, fasting is always to abstain from food or water for a distinct period of time. In Scripture, we never find anyone withholding from other things such as TV, gum, chocolate, etc. It is always the withholding of food and water that is the fuel for this particular weapon. Each of the weapons of warfare I am listing, including fasting, can be used for personal goals. But for our purposes today, I am speaking of fasting with a specific objective in mind, accompanied with intercessory prayer. Because there are times that we do not understand circumstances surrounding a certain objective, we can fast to obtain clarity. The Bible gives us several instances in both Old Testament and New Testament where fasting was key to hearing from the Lord and providing direction in a spiritual battle. One of the main purposes of this type of fasting is to bring us to a place of intense focus. As we fast regarding a specific target, our viewpoint becomes rather concentrated on the target of our prayer. When we fast, it is not to make the outcome go in our favor or direct circumstances in a manner we choose. When we fast, it is to hear God's directive, obtain understanding, and point our prayer in such a way that it could potentially change the result of the situation.

Remember that fasting has the potential to bring results that could come by no other means. When we fast, we are outwardly displaying the fact that we are inwardly saying this circumstance is more important than even sustenance to ourselves. We may not always be able to change the outcome as a result of our fasting, but we will receive clarity and understanding as a result. When the Old Testament character, Daniel, was faced with overwhelming circumstances, he fasted and prayed until the angel of the Lord was able to interpret the situation for him. This understanding of the context for Daniel came through a heavenly messenger. That messenger was an angel sent by God to help Daniel, which rolls us into the next weapon of our study.

One weapon that modern believers often negate in their times of intercession are the angels. For whatever reason, these heavenly hosts have been marginalized in the modern era. So important are these beings to the battle that their presence is mentioned in Scripture over one hundred times. Although we as human beings do not command angels, they are sent to minister to us and to battle Satan directly on our behalf. If you would like an in-depth study on these heavenly hosts, one of the best resources to read on the subject of angels was written in the 1970's by the Rev. Billy Graham. His book on the subject of angels explains the activity and purposes of these celestial beings in a way that stays true to biblical context.

As I mentioned earlier, although we do not command the angels, we (our prayers) can certainly affect their activity. Let me point out that there are times when angels are directed by the Lord to do things just because He is sovereign and just, but the majority of the time, the activity or inactivity is a direct result of our prayer. One point to illustrate this is that Satan cannot kill you, or he would have done it a long time ago. He does not possess the power or authority to usurp God's sovereign will. But he does possess the ability to fill the void when you and I do not pick up our weapons and fight. Whether it is a general lie or direct influence of demonic forces that affect human behavior, unless the church is praying offensively, Satan will win the battle. When God's people begin to pray for a situation, the angels are dispatched accordingly. If we are not specific in our prayers, it can produce delays; or if we quit before results are achieved, it can mean that we never see the kingdom prevail. No wonder Satan is constantly distracting the church and fostering passivity within our ranks!

The last weapon we want to look at today is the gift of tongues or praying in the Spirit. So effective is this weapon that it has been fought continually throughout the ages. I believe there are many sectors within the body of Christ who do not utilize this weapon because they have no context for its importance and have not been taught the value of this gift. You see, when we pray in tongues, we are allowing the Spirit of God to pray through us. This is key because God does not directly inhabit this realm of the heavenlies we call earth. This jurisdiction has been left for you and me to steward properly and to fill it with inhabitants that will bring glory to the Lord. Those inhabitants have the unique ability through Christ to not only allow the Holy Spirit to dwell inside them, but to have the Holy Spirit pray through them. This is what we, Pentecostals/Charismatics, often call the baptism in the Holy Spirit. It is the ability through the gift of speaking in tongues that we allow the Spirit of God to pray through us. Nothing could be more central to this battle than God Himself to speak into it. This weapon of our warfare can be deployed for several different tactics to destroy the enemy.

Romans 8:26–27 states, "Likewise the Spirit also helps in our weaknesses. For we do not know what we should pray for as we ought, but the Spirit Himself makes intercession for us with groaning which cannot be uttered. Now He who searches the hearts knows what the mind of the Spirit is, because He makes intercession for the saints according to the will of God."

What better way to express God's determination for a situation than to have the Spirit of God speak through us and into that situation.

In conclusion, let me say that when we begin to apply the weapons of our warfare against the enemy directly, it changes everything. Understanding these gifts is only the first step to victory in our homes, churches, and communities. I would challenge you to take an evaluation of this armory and put these weapons to work in the places you occupy.

> *Father, we give you thanks that you have not left us without the resources to fight our adversary. You have given us every tool we need to engage in the heavenly battle. Father, we ask that you allow us the grace to learn and the ability to continue when we grow weary.*
> *Amen.*

CHAPTER 7

PULLING BACK THE VEIL

Finally, my brethren, be strong in the Lord and in the power of His might. Put on the whole armor of God, that you may be able to stand against the wiles of the devil. For we do not wrestle against flesh and blood, but against principalities, against powers, against the rulers of the darkness of this age, against spiritual hosts of wickedness in the heavenly places.

—Ephesians 6:10–12

If you and I could pull back the veil of our flesh to see that which is unseen, what do you think we would find? In this chapter, I hope to address this question while staying true to a biblical context for spiritual warfare. Because the lines can sometimes become gray surrounding the subject, we will also address tactics the enemy uses to distract. Our intentions are that you would be able to distinguish between what is really going on in the heavenlies and what is just a diversion the enemy is using to keep a foothold in the situation. As the apostle Paul mentions in the above scripture, this is not flesh and blood we are contending with in our struggle for dominance. Jesus Christ taken the keys of hell and the grave only to place them into the hands of His church. Satan's goal is to keep us occupied with temporal problems in order that he may continue to enjoy occupying our place of authority. It is important to remember that in the absence of true authority, something or someone will always fill the vacuum. That is where you and I, as believers in Jesus Christ, must take responsibility for the spiritual well-being of our homes, churches, and communities. Granted that this is a lofty goal if we did not have the resource to accomplish the task but with Christ as our Mediator, anything is possible.

You see there are two main sources in the heavenlies that fuel the angelic battles during this present age we in which we live. First, that Christ is interceding for those who come to Him and call on His name. Second, that Satan is constantly accusing those same people and working diligently to produce mindsets of shame, guilt, or heaviness. Let us take some time to explore these two activities and analyze how we can effectively change the spiritual atmosphere surrounding us. I sometimes like to point out that there are two types of Christians—thermometers and thermostats. A thermometer is a person who sees everyone and everything only to continually tell us what is happening. This approach to the spiritual is more attune to a broadcast commentator rather than a kingdom soldier. But a thermostat is someone who not only sees and knows what is spiritually happening but chooses to change the atmosphere rather than except things as they are. These are the ones that choose to confront the enemy rather than passively watch the world go by.

Part 1: Ears to Hear

In the realm of the spirit, there is plenty of chatter going on. Between Jesus interceding, the enemy accusing, and our own mind, it can sometimes feel as though we need caller ID for the voices in our heads. Hopefully in this chapter we can help you sort some of those things out. Just having a basic knowledge of what the heavenlies look and sound like will help you discern the root of what you hear when you listen in. If you haven't been listening at all, perhaps this will become inspiration for you to be more observant. If we could not "pray continually," then the Scripture would not have instructed us to do so.

Although there are several verses throughout the Bible that give us a glimpse into the unseen realm of the spirit, there are two in particular that I would like to highlight for our study today.

The first is that Hebrews chapter 7:25 tells us that Jesus has taken the position of high priest and now lives to intercede for those who come to Him. In short, Jesus is now the mediator between humanity and the Father. He intercedes as our high priest, and He rules as the King of kings. The term *intercession*, as used in Scripture, means that Christ Himself intervenes in the lives of those that call upon Him or have their situation brought before Him by someone else. As the church, our role in this priestly ministry, is to be a people who can join in with those that are calling out on the name of Jesus and stand in the gap for those that are captive to this present darkness.

One of the most critical activities you and I can participate in is having a prayer life that responds to those around us rather than being consumed by our own circumstances. That is not to say that we never bring our own problems before the Lord, but it is to say that our SELVES should not be central to our prayer lives. Sad to say that a great deal of the Holy Spirit's energy is spent motivating us to align with what Christ is actually doing as our high priest. If you have been following this series of teachings, it now should become clear to you why I took so much time explaining the veil of our flesh and the trappings of this world. Unless you have allowed God to deal with your selfishness, going before Him on other people's behalf will seem wasteful to you. As you become a receptive vessel, willing to be used by God to hear these petitions of others and respond accordingly, you realize that this is our greatest contribution as citizens of the kingdom in this present life.

The second scripture I would like to expound on today is found in Revelations 12:7–17. In this passage, we find that Satan, the accuser, has been cast out of heaven as a result of Christ's victory on the cross. Not only has Satan been denied the access to God's throne, but he has also taken one-third of the angelic hosts with him that must remain under darkness until the judgment. That darkness is found not only in the spiritual realm surrounding the earth but the earth itself. Having been cast out of the place of their original habitation, they must now find a liaison to accomplish the task of accusing the brethren before the Lord. It is a common misconception that Satan has the ability to stand before our God or to come and go as he pleases. I mentioned earlier in this writing that Satan cannot work apart from darkness. The moment he comes into the light, he will be destroyed. Because God is light, it stands to reason that Satan has no place in the immediate vicinity of the throne. It is in the context of this dilemma that I would like to make a point. Satan knows that there is now only one vehicle for his accusations to reach the judge of all the earth—that is through those who have been redeemed by the blood of the Lamb. As a new creation in Christ, you and I have the unique ability to come and go from this present world to the throne of grace. It is through us and the words of our mouth that the enemy must do his best to manipulate. The concept I am presenting to the church is that instead of you and I aligning ourselves with the intercessions of our King, we become an instrument of accusation that allies with the enemy and his attempt to slander. Thousands of times each day there are self-motivated prayers spoken before God's holy throne in an attempt to sway the Lord into aligning with our agendas. Because this is a doctrine that is new to most, we can take a moment to illustrate this point further. The enemy knows that the words of our mouth are a powerful instrument. Proverbs tells us that the power of life and death are found in the tongue. James also alerts us to the importance of wrangling our vocal cords and that little member called the tongue. Jesus warned us we will be accounted for the words we speak.

Because our words have such potential for life and death, the enemy is constantly trying to use them as part of his scheme. With this in view, we will transition into a subject I feel bears examination.

Part 2: Playing Defense

One of the best things to remember regarding spiritual warfare is "the enemy knows that a good offense is his best defense."

Satan's oldest trick in the book is to get you offended. Proverbs says that a brother offended is harder to win than a strong city. It is imperative that we guard our heart against the root of offense that comes from the enemy. The Greek wording for this is *skandalon* which means "to entrap or stumble." While it is true that we need not create offense, it is equally as important to not take on offense. Satan is a master at setting a snare for us to fall into in regard to offense. If he can get you to distrust someone or question their motives, he can usually plant seeds for future offense. One way we take on offense is when we listen to someone else's opinion instead of God's opinion about the character of another person. Another is prejudice against people groups or religious doctrines. This sets up a classic maneuver for the enemy to drive a wedge into our relationships without hearing God's heart on the person or subject at hand.

One example found in Scripture is when all of Jesus's disciples forsook Him as He was taken prisoner by the temple guard in Gethsemane. After three and a half years of being with Jesus, seeing the miraculous, and leaving all to follow, these men still did not have a way to process the path Christ would take to the cross. Not only was this scenario testing their present relationship with God but testing everything they had been taught culturally about the Messiah. Our preconceived ideas about who God is and what He will do can become a foothold for the enemy if we aren't careful. This is why the weapon of humility is so crucial to the battle. As followers of Christ, we must not fall prey to presumption. There is no opportunity for the Lord to give you understanding, heal your heart, or take you to the next season if you are offended.

Father, may we be aware of the enemy's schemes to trap us into passivity and offense. Let us walk closely to you in the days ahead. May our hearts stay in tune with you plans and purposes for the sake of the kingdom. In the mighty name above all names, Jesus Christ. Amen.

CHAPTER 8

JESUS CHRIST, THE "MESSIAH"

But you Bethlehem, in the land of Judah, are not the least among the rulers of Judah; For out of you shall come a Ruler Who will shepherd my people Israel.

—Matthew 2:6

A book on understanding the heavens could never be complete without a portion dedicated to the King and His kingdom. Throughout these writings, we have emphasized Jesus Christ in His role as our high priest and what that priestly ministry looks like when functioning appropriately. In this section, I would like to take time to highlight Jesus as king and ruler over all of creation. Without this revealing of Christ's role as king, it can place us in the crosshairs of offense towards God Himself or prompt us to question His goodness and trustworthiness.

There have been countless situations that I personally witnessed throughout the course of my spiritual life where individuals or whole groups have become upset at God for what He did or did not do regarding circumstances that directly affected them. When it comes to our comprehension of Jesus Messiah, it will serve us well to remember two things. First, that God has a different timetable than us. Second, that He is sovereign over all of creation and not just our circumstance. These ideas we are about to explain might be, to our traditional perspective, a paradigm shift from the ideas of who Jesus is as we read in the Gospels. Just as the Jews struggled with the idea of the Messiah being a suffering servant in order to redeem humanity, we can also have a hard time comprehending Jesus as anything but the suffering servant. According to Scripture, He is now at the right hand of God and will rule forever. Don't mistake what I am presenting to you in this teaching. I would never diminish the Master's role as the Lamb of God. But the truth of it is that He is the King of kings and the Lord of lords. And according to the revelation that John experienced, might I tell you that this is the mindset we need to develop of Christ. He has eyes of fire and a sword in His mouth (Rev 19:11–16). My personal opinion is that we tend to keep Him placed in that role of Lamb so that we remain comfortable.

The closer we draw to the end of the age, we perhaps need to sharpen our viewpoint on Jesus the King. Because this is the role that will bear the most significance in the end times, it is the role that the book on end times (Revelations) emphasizes more than any other. Jesus as king and judge over creation includes His ability to control the heavenlies and dominate His enemies. These are the things that matter most as we wrap up the modern era. This does not diminish the redemption of mankind but allows us to comprehend what God's focus is as we move into the last days. As a matter of fact, there will be a tremendous harvest of souls during the midst of these battles.

Part 1: God's Timetable

To understand certain aspects about the Lord and perhaps answer questions regarding His actions or lack of we must consider the "otherness" of God; that God is in no way like us when He makes decisions. The idea here is that to walk with the Lord we must become aware that He is not like us in His ways, thinking, or timetable. A lack of this understanding can surely lead us down a path that either creates an idol in our minds or promotes the thought that God is not real. To form an idol in our minds is to reduce God to the level of humanity. To promote the idea that God does not exist will set us on a course for destruction. The fool says there is no God.

UNDERSTANDING THE HEAVENS

While it is okay to wonder why God is apparently slow to act, this way of thinking takes us down an erosive slope to self-absorption. To continually question God is to continually put yourself in the place of God, and sooner or later, your heart becomes hard to the King and His kingdom, a.k.a. pharaoh syndrome.

Understanding God's timetable can sometimes be as simple as understanding the principles behind how and when God acts upon situations. One of the greatest principles I have personally learned throughout the years came through a good friend and mentor, Al Houghton. For further study on this subject, Al has written several books that include the information I am about to share (WordatWork.org).

This principle unlocked several keys to the kingdom for me, as well as an understanding of God's timetable. This is the principle of *fullness*. This comes from a group of Hebrew/Greek words that let us in on the how, when, and why God works when acting in a situation. Galatians 4:4 says that in the fullness of time, Jesus came to the earth. Jesus declares to the religious rulers that they would fill up the measure of their father's guilt in Matthew 23:32. And in Genesis 15:13–16, the Lord tells Abram that He is promising a piece of land, but he would have to wait until the time of the Amorites is full. This principle of fullness is found throughout the Scripture but has somehow been neglected by most of us who study God's word faithfully. For me this doctrine answers plenty of questions regarding the otherness of God.

You see, as the judge of all, Jesus must be sightless to our personal gain or to our suffering and act according to righteousness. In this passage from Genesis 15, the Lord explains to Abram that his offspring would be slaves for four hundred years and then He would judge. No matter how much prayer and crying out to God they did, until that time was complete, they weren't coming out of that situation. The same goes for the possession of the land of Canaan, until the Amorites had filled the land with iniquity, God could not and would not take the land from them and give to another. In our Western mindset, somehow we believe that God will go against righteous judgement and favor us personally. This is why we have a hard time understanding this principle because we have been taught that God is merciful but have neglected to teach that He is just. As humans, we have a hard time looking at both sides or in this case, multiple facets to what is happening in a situation.

Through the years, this doctrine being embedded in my soul has helped as my family, and I have navigated through the path of life. By sharing this concept, I hope that you would grasp hold of this truth and ask the Lord to reveal to you what is happening in each situation that you pray for or go through personally.

Part 2: God's Sovereignty

Staying on track with the theme that God is other than we are, I want to present to you the fact that God is sovereign. This means that He is the ruler of all creation and does not need to ask permission or seek out authority to act when all that He does is just and righteous. God's sovereignty allows Him to be the only one to act alone and according to His own will (Eph 1:5).

As ruler of all, the Lord has a divine plan that will always go according to the way He has established. There are two things to be drawn from this statement. Nothing can change this eternally instituted story He has written, and we cannot sit idly by as this plan is being unfolded before our eyes. Our role is to seek out what the Lord is doing, hopefully connect on the right timetable, and pray the prayers that will shore up the redemption of those called to it. To put it in layman's terms, you have no way of stopping certain events and seasonal changes that come upon the earth. This can seem contrary to what we talked about in chapter 6 on being a thermostat, but that is why we continued into this teaching. You must know the Lord, have fellowship with the Spirit, and discern what and what not to put effort into. You see, in the last days, there will be persecution and suffering like the world has never known, and that season will usher in the Second Coming of Jesus Christ. In the midst of this most horrendous time, God will have a church that can stand in the face of adversity with a holy boldness like never before. This is the part that might pull you from your comfort zone. In the Last Days, the Lord will place emphasis on destroying those that directly oppose His plan and His kingdom. If we are uncomfortable with this view of Jesus, then it may be time to start praying for the wisdom necessary to endure and thrive in such a season. Fear not because God has not forsaken His people even though it may appear that way at times. To understand God's sovereignty is to also understand that He has us in the cradle of His hand and refuses to allow the enemy to utterly destroy us. Those that are called by His name will not be taken from Him. This is the mystery of His love for you and me.

> *For I am convinced that neither death nor life, nor Angel nor principalities nor powers, nor things present nor things to come, nor height nor depth, nor any other created thing shall be able to separate us from the love of God which is in Christ Jesus our Lord.*
>
> —Romans 8:38–39

CONCLUSION

To wrap things up, let me mention again that the war for the human soul will continue until the Lord returns for His church. But in the meantime, you and I are challenged to occupy or carry on the family business. As previously stated, that business is the redemption of humanity and destroying the work of our enemy.

A scripture from Psalm 110 that is frequently mentioned in the New Testament says, "The Lord said to my Lord, sit at my right hand, until I make your enemies your footstool."

Sometimes, in the heat of battle, it seems as though things will never turn in your favor. But let this scripture be a reminder that our God has the final say and will eventually overcome all of His enemies. It is important for us to keep in mind that all of creation is part of the kingdom and not just what affects me personally. It is easy for us to get encumbered by the circumstances we can see on a daily basis. But the kingdom of God includes millions of those circumstances every day. As I write these words, I realize that most of my readers have never been taught that kingdom life is a life lived for others and not for oneself. Every year, we teach these principles, but it seems as though the church is becoming more and more self-absorbed. This is not a rebuke by any means but an observation from someone who sees the blank stares and fields the questions regarding how God could want us to live in such a way that could possibly mean individual or corporate suffering. As you and I mature in our faith, we should allow the Lord to direct us to the location, workplace, and relationships that are most beneficial for His kingdom. The apostle Peter, in one of his letters, speaks to us regarding the fact that Jesus showed him that he would die for the sake of the kingdom if he continued to follow after the Lord. He did it anyway (2 Pt 1:14).

May we become those that look not to the present age for comfort or affirmation but a people whose minds and hearts are fixed upon the age to come in which we can walk with the Lord unobstructed by any enemy.

ABOUT THE AUTHOR

After being called by God to leave a successful business career, Curtis Wilson has worked in apostolic ministry for over twenty years to places such as the Mississippi Delta and the Navajo Indian reservation. Having witnessed the first-hand need for teaching material, which goes beyond nominal topics, he launched SeriouswithGod.org. From this platform, he hopes to inspire, equip, and release a generation of devoted Jesus-followers. Curtis and his wife, Tabitha, live in Farmerville, Louisiana, with their two children, Rayna and Jacob. He loves the outdoors, cooking, and building things with his hands.